AF573751

THE BATSFORD COLOUR BOOK OF SUSSEX

Introduction and commentaries by
Judith Glover

B. T. BATSFORD LTD LONDON

First published 1975

Filmset by Servis Filmsetting Ltd, Manchester
Printed and bound in Great Britain by
Morrison & Gibb Ltd, Edinburgh
for the publishers B. T. Batsford Ltd, 4 Fitzhardinge Street, London W1
and 23 Cross Street, Brookvale, NSW 2100, Australia
ISBN 0 7134 2814 7

Contents

Acknowledgments

The Publishers are grateful to the following for supplying colour transparencies reproduced in this book:

Noel Habgood for pages 19, 25, 29, 39, 41, 43, 45, 51, 57 and 61
A. F. Kersting for pages 27, 47, 49, 55 and 59
P. W. Lang for page 33
Kenneth Scowen for pages 17, 21, 23, 31, 35, 37, 53 and 63

Introduction

I think it may be truthfully said that no county – as no country – can be all things to all men; but to my mind Sussex comes closer to this ideal than most. Except in its fortunate lack of heavy industrial communities it is a microcosm of England, that England of which poets used to sing (and more poets have sung of Sussex than of any county, surely), but of which there has now become less and less worth singing about.

Sussex is rather like an island within an island: to get to it from the Metropolis is a definite act. The traveller into Kent or Surrey makes the transition without really noticing, no longer more than vaguely aware of where the administrators would have him believe London ends and those counties begin – if such is any longer the case. Sussex is different, buffered from the Greater London sprawl by those two counties and enjoying definite boundaries with both, as it does with Hampshire to the west.

The reason for this insularity is not only geographical but historical: a relic of the days, not so many centuries ago, when the vast Weald, that flat lowland basin between the northern boundary and the sweeping rampart of the South Downs beyond which lie the coastal plain and the English Channel, was so thickly forested as to make it virtually impenetrable. Those who needed to travel from London to any place along the Sussex coast had to rely upon relays of guides to lead them through dense forests of oak where not only wild cats and wolves roamed, but human predators too. The difficulties of journeying were made even greater by the nature of the terrain itself. The Wealden land is heavy, acidic clay, ideal for growing oak trees then, and grain now, but extremely difficult to travel over in the days before roads were metalled. It could take literally weeks to accomplish a journey along one of these primitive tracks, sinking repeatedly into the mire on the way; and if a load of any weight were being transported by 'tugs', or sledges, laboriously hauled by teams of oxen, there could be a complete bog-down, which meant precious time wasted in getting both animals and load out of the thick, clinging mud. There are tales of well over a year being needed for a load of pig-iron to reach London from the iron foundries of the Weald.

So Sussex tended to be left alone by its English neighbours in earlier centuries, though less so by its Continental ones. In prehistoric times, of course, it had been physically one with Northern France, a continuing land mass until, perhaps 8,000 years ago, some great sea surge from the north forced further apart the banks of the river which ran down the centre of this broad plain, creating a funnel for strong tides to gush violently through and complete the work of forming the sea barrier of which England has frequently had cause to be thankful since.

By the time the Channel was formed Sussex was already inhabited, though not numerously. Stone Age tribes from Europe seem to have wandered this way, no doubt led on by game they were hunting: relics of their implements and the bones of the animals they had caught have been found, particularly in the area of the Western Rother valley.

The separation of England from the European land mass seems to have halted colonisation for some considerable time until the Neolithic people, who had landed further west in England, came eastward into what is now Sussex, settling largely on the Downs, no doubt delighted to find there an abundant source of the flints they needed for making weapons and domestic tools. Many traces of their mine workings are still to be found on the Downs.

Later incursions, though, came directly from seaward. The Bronze Age Beaker Folk – their name derives from their distinctively flat-bottomed drinking vessels – preferred the flat coastal plain and the Weald to the Downs, and went in for livestock farming. Then, after something like a century and a half of settlement by them and by the Celts, and a subsequent mingling together to form a people we call the Britons, there arrived the Romans to establish a centre for overseas trade on a now-vanished peninsula near the present Chichester, itself regarded as the most important centre in this part of the island and linked to Londinium by one of the great Roman roads, Stane Street.

The Roman occupation has left indelible marks on the Sussex we know today. The huge castle at Pevensey (then Anderida) was built to serve as their principal military garrison in the county. Modern Chichester covers no-one knows what treasures of Roman building; while the partially excavated palace at Old Fishbourne and the villa at Bignor are among the finest relics of that distant, benign conquest, which bestowed benefits unappreciated by the invading Saxons, who, after the legions' departure, let the decorated villas throughout the county decay, the mosaic floors become overgrown, and the communications with London and elsewhere lapse. Sussex retreated into itself once more.

The arrival of Christianity, represented by St. Wilfred of Northumbria, who landed in 681 AD near Selsey, penetrated this isolation to some degree, and brought that town much importance, along with such new centres of craftsmanship as Lewes, Steyning and Hastings. Setbacks to further development were caused by marauding Danes – though we may be grateful to them now, since many of the wooden churches they destroyed in their raids were in due course replaced by stone Saxon churches whose foundations have withstood the wear and tear of centuries and 'restoration'.

Seeking lasting peace from the terror, the Saxons elected a Dane to be their king. He was Cnut, known better to us as Canute. Just what the truth of the story of his trying in vain to command the waves to retreat (or did he try it because he *was* vain?) will never be known, nor can it be said for sure where it happened – if happen it did. A strong claimant, though, is Bosham, where he had a palace in which it is believed his eight-year-old daughter died: the skeleton of a young child was found enclosed in a stone coffin in Bosham church in the mid-nineteenth century, at the spot where traditionally Canute's daughter was buried.

Saxon influence on Sussex was immense, not only in giving it its name (from the *Sūðseaxe*, or South Saxons, who conquered it during the fifth century), but in creating the very pattern of the county, its people's way of life, and its styles of building, derived from European origins. It is said to possess three Saxon treasures still – the churches of Bosham, Sompting and Worth – but there are many minor treasures too, and traces of further ones already discovered or yet to be found. This is great hunting ground for archaeologists, whatever their period of interest.

Bosham has a further significant part to play in the county's story – and indeed, in the history of England: it was from there that the future King Harold sailed in 1064. Had he not been shipwrecked on the French coast, and bound himself loyally to the service of William of Normandy, only to return to England to accept the crown, William might not have mounted the punitive expedition which was to result in the conquest of England. Visitors who come to Hastings to look for the site of the battle will not find it. It lies a little inland at a pretty town named Battle in its memory; though Hastings suffered from fire and sword as the Normans, who had landed at Pevensey, made their way through to overcome inferior forces whose only advantage was a strong defensive position.

There is something of a dichotomy about the attitude of Sussex folk towards the battle whose outcome would, unbeknown to anyone at the time, result in profound and lasting influence upon English political, religious, social and cultural life, not to mention upon its very language and its dynastic heritage. The battle itself was, after all, a resounding defeat for the home side. Much that the occupation introduced ran counter to what had been traditionally acceptable to Anglo-Saxon attitudes, and was to cause ferment which to this day has never quite subsided. Yet it was a momentous event in English history; and it happened in Sussex. Nine centuries later there was some heat to be felt in the county from argument between those who planned the 1966 celebrations of the anniversary of the invasion, and those who reminded them that it was not a matter for celebration at all.

Perhaps it would have been smoother if someone had suggested that it be celebrated as the last *successful* invasion of our shore; for it was. Countless hit-and-run raids have occurred since, mostly mounted by the Dutch or French, and to a large extent against Sussex, which suffered more physical damage and loss of life from them than most other places put together. But those other great contenders for conquest, Napoleonic France and Nazi Germany, couldn't manage it. Had they even reached these shores they would have found the prepared defences of Sussex, and the determination of its people, as stubborn an opposition as they could have expected anywhere.

Incidentally, it's a whimsical sidelight on the major issues of history that Pevensey Castle, built as a Roman defence against the Saxons, further fortified by the Normans against any comers, and manned against the arrival of the Spanish Armada, should in the Second World War have become an important local headquarters for that homespun force of diehard veterans, the Home Guard. There is something typical in that to me of a county whose men like it to be known of them that they 'won't be druv'.

An early action of the Normans, to find out just what they had acquired in conquering England, was to compile the great Domesday survey in 1086. It told them how many people lived in an area, a town, a hamlet; what was the predominant local industry or craft; how the whole formed patterns which could be moulded into tidily administered divisions.

Sussex presented a fairly clear-cut picture of six vertical segments, extending from the northern border to the sea, which the Normans called Rapes (the origin of the term is unknown). There were the combined Rapes of Chichester and Arundel, then Bramber, Lewes, Pevensey and Hastings. Each had its capital town, complete with castle, guarding the coast or a vital stretch of the five principal Sussex rivers: Arun, Adur, Ouse, Cuckmere and Eastern Rother. Many centuries later Sussex would be further divided into smaller segments under the provisions of the Enclosures Act; then, as now, into two, East and West Sussex with their respective 'capitals', Lewes and Chichester – though the latter should perhaps have pre-eminence, being the more ancient and possessing the county's only cathedral.

But then, people have always been dividing Sussex into theoretical patterns for one purpose or another. There are those, for instance, who would place it under a sort of grid, formed vertically by the major roads from London and laterally by the cross country routes; or by the canals and, later, the railways. It's a game anyone may play, and my own version of it produces two Sussexes – inland Sussex and Sussex-by-the-sea – divided principally by the long line of the South Downs (whose many devotees would consider to be a separate Sussex in their own right).

Of course, it's good old Sussex-by-the-sea of which those who have never been near the county have heard, and which is also most familiar to those who come as visitors. From, or through, London the vast majority of these travel, borne by train or coach or car. The first of my two Sussexes for them is merely a blur of scenery that is softer, greener and less spoiled than that of so much of Britain, dotted with picturesque old villages and hamlets (the 'roses-round-the-door' image of the English cottage comes very much to life in Sussex), fine period houses, many of them half-timbered, pretty pubs, quaint little shops which look as though they might still have pre-war stock on their shelves, and doubtless sometimes have; contented sheep and cows, a good proportion of horses, and a great acreage of grain.

It is with impatience, though, that these travellers view such things. They are journeying with an objective, which is not attained until the Downs are topped or cut through, and there lies the sea, back-lit in silver by the sun. William Cobbett, who did a lot of riding around the county in the 1820s, remarked on the difficulty of getting anyone to believe that one might wish to travel other than by the most direct turnpike road: 'they think you mad if you express your wish to avoid turnpike roads, and a great deal more than half mad if you talk of going even from necessity by any other road'.

It's a well known characteristic of the modern excursionist that he prefers to feed himself into the route most chosen by his fellows, all preferring to accompany the well-signposted herd even at the cost of wearying congestion and delays, rather than adventure with a map. I would not deny that the Sussex coast has its magnetic charm: to a great extent it has suffered less unsightly development than many other coastal areas of Britain, though it has its lamentable stretches. But if my two Sussexes do exist, and the one draws the crowds, oblivious for the most part to the nature and essence of the resort itself, rather than to the combination of sea, beach and commercial amusements which might be anywhere else, not necessarily in Sussex, the other remains more secret, more unspoiled, less appreciated. It's a pity, and yet a relief. It is thereby kept reasonably intact for the connoisseur, the resident, the adventurous; for those who prefer the quiet of a country lane winding down through green fields towards a huddle of thatched roofs to the noise of a crowded beach where multi-coloured bodies lie out in the mid-day sun. If the sea-seekers did begin to pause in any numbers to show an interest in those quiet places off the south-bound roads, the ever watchful commercial developer would scent something in the air, and the money-men and their architects and surveyors would move smoothly in.

Undoubtedly, inland Sussex has a great deal to offer anyone with an eye for natural beauty, antiquity and the good old values of life. There are hundreds of little vistas in Sussex comparable with some of those so tourist-thronged during the summer months that they cease to be vistas at all. The best of them have been discovered and are visited, although in minute numbers compared with the multitude who wander the seafronts.

I am thinking, for example, of the great houses, blending history with graciousness and art, such as Petworth and Uppark; the noble castles, in settings of most unwarlike beauty, such as Bodiam, Herstmonceux, Pevensey and Amberley; the churches, from the welcoming informality of Chichester Cathedral to those imposing structures at Lancing College and Arundel (the Victorian Gothic Roman Catholic church), to the quiet little country ones, mustily redolent of great age and neglected faith, always seeming to be waiting for Evensong.

There are antique mysteries, exemplified by the Long Man of Wilmington. Who is this gigantic figure, carved in the chalk of Windover Hill, his arms outstretched to grasp – what? No one knows what the poles signify, and probably, despite argument, no-one ever will; but it doesn't matter, if to get a look at him the unsuspecting visitor is tempted to the top of the velvet-coated Downs, where the views are superb, the air almost makes the head spin, and there is the temptation to leave the car down below and promptly tramp off along the whole 80 miles of the South Downs Way, which runs from beyond the Hampshire border to Beachy Head.

Beachy Head itself is one of Britain's greatest vantage points, from where, almost 600 feet above a rock-strewn shore, one may follow the undulating line of the Seven Sisters cliffs, white as the chalk they are, towards Cuckmere Haven. Should the day not be clear and the mists come swirling up from the sea, there is a glorious spectacle of writhing shapes heaping and humping as the wind blows them and the sun colours them from behind. Beachy Head is said to have its ghost, luring people to their death down that sheer drop which many, alas, have taken; and I can almost believe in such a ghost, having seen those beckoning swirling mist-figures for myself.

But then, they do believe in ghosts in parts of Sussex; and in fairies – 'pharisees' as they called them widely once. Away from the main road and the crowd, in many a quietly rustling coppice, or in the depths of a remnant of an ancient forest, or alone in a twisty, overgrown lane at dusk, it is perfectly easy to share such beliefs. Didn't Rudyard Kipling write *Rewards and Fairies* and some of his most enchanting and enchanted tales about the part of the county in which he lived, at Bateman's, one of the grandest of the houses built by the wealthy iron masters in the days when – it's hard to believe now – Sussex was the 'Black Country' of England, and its forests were being denuded to feed the fires of forges making the Navy's cannon, or to be shaped into masts and spars?

Many literary men have lived in Sussex, have deliberately sought out homes here as though drawn to it by that mystery of which literary inspiration is a part. They are gratefully remembered: Kipling by Bateman's and his earlier house at Rottingdean; Hilaire Belloc by his perfectly preserved windmill at Shipley; Henry James by Lamb House at Rye; and many more. But not all the mysteriousness of Sussex is attributable to the 'unknown': a lot of it was quite deliberately manufactured by those now romantic but then ruthless ruffians, the smugglers, or 'owlers' as they were called in Sussex dialect speech.

Five and twenty ponies, trotting through the dark,
Brandy for the parson, baccy for the clerk . . .

Thus Kipling epitomised the attitude of Sussex folk to the 'gentlemen' who ran their contraband deep into the county in times when it was both prudent to turn a blind eye, and tactful to give them assistance, at the risk of their violence if they were opposed. They were gangsters in a popular cause, evading unpopular taxes, all but ruling towns like Alfriston and Rye in the process, and leaving their memory in the form of secret passages, concealed cellars, and other ingenious places of hiding or means of escape in many an old house still standing to be pointed out with affectionate reference to them.

The smugglers are gone – almost; the iron industry is gone too, leaving the once forested areas to be used for crop growing; the great castles slumber as tourist attractions. Yet Sussex is no backwater that has opted out of modern life: proud though it is to have preserved more of its traditional crafts than almost any other county, even if their practice is now limited, it has moved with the times, and continues to do so. Once those notorious mud lanes through the Weald were transformed into good hard-surfaced roads, and the Prince Regent and his set had discovered the benefits and delights of sea bathing and disporting themselves on the race tracks across the Downs behind Brighton, development of the coast proceeded swiftly, yet tastefully; and amongst the more deplorable structures attributable to the twentieth century there remain many delightful reminders of Regency style and taste, to give the Sussex resorts enviable character amongst the commercialism. And amongst themselves they are infinitely variable: Eastbourne still shows a face of Edwardian elegance; Hastings Old Town climbs crookedly up the high hill surmounted by the ruins of its Norman castle; Worthing still clings to its Victorian primness; and Brighton . . . well, Brighton stands or falls, according to the eye of the beholder.

Many books have been written on Sussex and, indeed, it requires a book to list its assets, modern and historical, and assess its qualities. I can only mention in passing such other outstanding features as its cultural contribution to British life – the internationally respected and unique opera house at Glyndebourne, the thriving theatres at Chichester, Brighton and elsewhere; the sporting and recreational facilities: Goodwood race course, show jumping at Hickstead, the lovely Saffrons cricket ground at Hove, the superb sailing harbour of Chichester, and, soon to come, Europe's biggest artificial yachting marina at Brighton. Good riding, walking and even motoring are all here for the enthusiasts;

and good pubs and restaurants too.

Sussex has something – more than one thing – for most of us, but above all for me at least a generally unspoiled character to be found less and less elsewhere in this overcrowded island. Inevitably, this will prove a diminishing quality. The population is increasing, meaning more building and the disappearance of more and more open land. Overspill schemes are bringing tens of thousands of displaced Londoners into the county. One has only to look at the rapid growth of Crawley, already containing far more people than had been originally envisaged, and with the biggest industrial estate in Sussex where previously there had been only a village, to wonder whether this is not the thin end of the wedge. Growing congestion in Kent and Surrey may bring many refugees across the border; while the increasing longevity of Britons will swell the demand for retirement homes which can only be supplied by expanding some of those 'sunset' towns along the coast. Coastal reclamation plans are being prepared; but inland development is inescapable.

Fortunately this is an age of growing awareness of the vital necessity to offset such pressures by guidance from visionary planners and conservation groups. Sussex is especially rich in the latter, and though they may not possess the money and the steamroller influence of the developers, their advice has often proved more than useful to local authorities. It may just be that the flood tide of conservationism is coming in time to save the best of Sussex for posterity, and at least modify the transformation that the rest of it cannot hope to escape.

The Plates

RYE

Marooned high on a hill of sandstone, rising dramatically from the flat fenland, Rye was once a thriving seaport, one of the original Cinque Ports. The sea has receded some two miles by now but the fishing fleet still reaches it by way of the Rother.

Its proximity to the sea made the medieval walled town especially vulnerable to French raiders, who burnt down most of it in 1377. Smugglers found it a natural landing point, and many picturesque houses in its up-and-down cobbled streets were honeycombed with linked cellars and attics, designed as escape routes. Mermaid Street, seen here, is the most celebrated example: the Mermaid Inn, on the right, was in fact the rendezvous of the vicious Hawkhurst Gang, and in fiction that of the smuggler-clergyman 'Dr. Syn'.

Today Rye is a tourist showplace with many craftwork potteries. It has long been a favourite haven for artists and writers.

The
Mermaid
Inn

THE SEVEN SISTERS

Sailors in the days of the first Elizabeth probably gave 'The Seven Sisters' their name. These arcs of chalk, up to 260 feet high, form one of the three cliff blocks guarding the Sussex coast from Seaford to Eastbourne: the others are Beachy Head, separated from The Sisters by Birling Gap, and Seaford Head, cut off by Cuckmere Haven.

From Birling Gap, pictured here with its coastguard cottages, The Seven Sisters undulate westward to Cuckmere Haven, beginning with the smallest height, Went Hill Brow, over which runs the Went Way, a prehistoric track; then follow Baily's Brow, Flagstaff Point, Brass Point, Rough Brow – which is the highest of the arcs – Short Brow and Haven Brow.

Split by frost, undercut and battered by waves, The Sisters are shrinking back from the sea by more than two feet a year, and the gaps between them are widening. Eventually, The Seven Sisters will completely divide to form separate headlands.

BRIGHTON: REGENCY HOUSES

Brighton means different things to different people: a sprawling mini-London, the haunt of the sophisticated and the phoney, over-provided with antique shops and boutiques; one of Britain's finest seaside resorts, with attractions ranging from the most vulgarly popular to the most cultural; a dormitory for well-off commuters to the capital, only an hour away. . . .

Undeniably, it is a great, living monument to the time of the Regency, when the Prince of Wales and his dandified following made it a centre of fashion and sport and the new practice of sea-bathing transformed it into England's principal watering-place.

It declined later, but gained new vitality between the World Wars which it has never lost, though at the cost of much 'redevelopment'. Fortunately, many Regency terraces such as this remain and are now jealously protected by those who love their town for all that is most tasteful about it.

LICENSED
EVER

BOSHAM

In the Bayeux Tapestry the future King Harold, last ruler of Saxon England, is shown feasting at his manor at Bosham; and it was from Quay Meadow, now a field at the tip of the village, that he embarked on his ill-fated visit to William of Normandy in 1064.

The Church of the Holy Trinity, whose small shingled spire rises above the clutter of waterside cottages, marks Bosham as the oldest site of Christianity in Sussex, since it was the first Christian church to be built here and is rightfully regarded as one of the county's three Saxon treasures.

Bosham stands on a peninsula jutting out into Chichester Harbour and has been termed the 'capital' of that designated area of outstanding natural beauty, so popular now with yachtsmen and birdwatchers. The earliest water sportsman seems to have been King Canute, who had a palace at Bosham: his unsuccessful attempt to control the waves probably took place on the foreshore here.

SHIPLEY: BELLOC'S MILL

Sussex once had windmills by the hundred. Of those remaining, a few still grind wholemeal flour, but most have become private houses, or shops, or are simply preserved for their beauty and interest.

Over the door of this fine wooden galleried smock mill at Shipley an inscription reads 'Let this be a memorial to Hilaire Belloc who garnered a harvest of wisdom and sympathy for young and old'. The poet and author who sang the praise of Sussex in some of his best loved verse lived in King's Land, the house next to the mill, from 1906 until his death in 1953, at the age of 83.

He had bought the house, the mill and five acres for £1,000, and ensured that the mill was kept in perfect preservation. It contains momentoes of him, but is interesting to visitors in its own right as one of the best examples of a windmill in the South of England.

UPPARK

Emma, Lady Hamilton, danced on a table here; and the Duke of Wellington reluctantly declined the house as a gift from the nation because the hill road to it would be too steep for his carriage-horses. H. G. Wells did his first writing in the kitchen, when his mother was housekeeper, and made Uppark 'Bladesover' in his novel *Tono Bungay*.

Uppark stands high on the South Downs above the village of South Harting on the Sussex-Hampshire border. It was built about 1690, but the interior is a pure reflection of the fine eighteenth century taste of Sir Matthew Fetherstonhaugh and his wife. Even the fabrics and wallpaper of rooms such as this White and Gold Saloon are in their original condition, having been restored by being washed in a special herbal solution prepared by Lady Meade-Fetherstonhaugh, whose late husband made over Uppark to the National Trust to enable the public to see its glories.

PEVENSEY CASTLE

Almost 5,000 British are said to have been massacred by the invading Saxons when they broke through the defences of Anderida in 491 AD. Many were refugees, fleeing before a pitiless enemy, but others were families who had made their home inside the huge Roman fortress.

Anderida was built during the third century as part of the Roman defences along the 'Saxon Shore'. Ten acres of land were enclosed within sturdy walls that served as strong foundations for later building by the Saxons – who renamed the fortress Pevensey – and the Normans: Count Robert de Mortain, half brother of the Conqueror, built his castle within the original walls.

At the time of the Spanish Armada threat further fortifications were added and a battery set up. One of the guns is still there. The defences were again renewed during the Second World War when the Home Guard moved in, giving Pevensey Castle a defensive history spanning seventeen centuries.

HASTINGS OLD TOWN

Unique in England is the group of tarred wooden sheds clustered on the shingle of 'The Stade' at the Old Town end of Hastings. They are net shops, used by fishermen for hanging and drying their nets, and perpetuate a design several centuries old.

Fishing is still of importance to Hastings – declared chief of the Cinque Ports in the twelfth century – so many of these tall, angular net shops remain in constant use. The fishermen's chapel of St. Nicholas, standing here amongst them, is now a museum, housing the last Hastings lugger, *Enterprise*, and other relics of the industry.

This part of the town lies at the foot of the high hill surmounted by the ruins of the Norman castle. Some quaint old houses can be found in the vicinity too; but for the most part Hastings is devoted to the role of popular holiday resort, which it began to assume in the mid-nineteenth century.

THE LONG MAN OF WILMINGTON

Mystery and controversy surround the Long Man, a figure 240 feet long cut into the side of Windover Hill near Wilmington, and the only such chalk carving on the Sussex Downs.

It is thought to be of great antiquity, even though no recorded mention of the Long Man is known before the eighteenth century. Some antiquarians believe it was made by the monks of a nearby priory, others think it to be of Roman origin depicting Constantine the Great; while still others argue that it represents a heathen sun god pushing aside the doors of darkness.

Almost certainly, the Long Man is of very great age, and does represent a god: recent archaeological finds in Kent have produced an almost identical figure on a buckle. Probably the chalk figure was made by those who used the prehistoric track which still runs over Windover Hill and leads eventually to Avebury, the great Neolithic capital in Wiltshire.

AMBERLEY

An essential element of Sussex's distinctive beauty and atmosphere of timelessness is its villages, many of them little spoiled and possessing carefully preserved houses and cottages of great age. A gem among them is Amberley, near Arundel: no more than two or three streets, each with its quota of immaculate dwellings, brick and flint built, half-timbered and thatched roofed.

For many centuries the manor house of Amberley was the palace of the Bishops of Chichester. In the fourteenth century one of them, anticipating attacks by French marauders up the River Arun, enlarged the house into a square-towered castle. The raiders never came, in due course the bishops departed, and the castle was allowed to decay – though romantically – still overlooked by the Church of St. Michael, reached by the *cul de sac* shown here.

The Arun has retreated too, but the neighbouring Amberley Wild Brooks remain notable for fishing and boating.

CHICHESTER

Chichester, the cathedral city of West Sussex, was originally Regnum, capital of the British tribe of Regnenses. The conquering Romans made it one of their forts and Noviomagus, as it became, was the terminal of Stane Street, running from London. Then came the Saxons, who destroyed the fort, rebuilt it, and renamed it yet again – this time after Cissa, who was appointed governor in 516 AD.

The cathedral is mainly Norman, with a spire said to be the only cathedral spire which is visible from the sea. The sixteenth-century Market Cross, shown here, standing at the junction of four roads known as the Pallants – which follow the original Roman road system – has been the setting for many fairs, its great canopy providing shelter for the stalls and market folk.

As late as 1889 Chichester had five different trade fairs each week, centred on the Market Cross. Now only one survives to continue the tradition.

ROYAL ARMS

MILTON STREET

The little farming village of Milton Street, viewed here from the South Downs, lies in the valley of the Cuckmere, the smugglers' river during the eighteenth and early nineteenth centuries. An underground passage half a mile long is believed to lead to the village from Wilmington Priory and to have been used by the 'owlers', as Sussex smugglers were called.

The Downs behind Milton Street offer splendid walking, both for the short-distance stroller using a car to reach a vantage point, or for the dedicated rambler with stout boots and stick. Much of the land in this area is unfenced and easily accessible from the roads.

With the opening of the South Downs Way, one of the country's finest stretches of footpath, it is now possible to walk the entire 80-mile long track along the Downs from Beachy Head to Buriton, across the Hampshire border, with magnificent views at many points as a reward.

WORTH CHURCH

The Church of St. Nicholas at Worth has been described as one of the three Saxon treasures of Sussex – the others are the churches of Bosham and Sompting. Its age shows in its exterior, decorated with vertical stone strips spaced out along the walls, a characteristic motif of eleventh-century Saxon architecture. Mercifully, Victorian 'restoration' has done little to change the appearance of this big ancient building.

Inside, the church is cruciform, with a high, wide nave; and though there has been additional building down the centuries the bold Saxon design can be plainly seen in the three great arches leading to the chancel and transepts.

The Forest of Worth, to the south, takes its name from the village and supplied the Sussex iron industry in this area with its timber during the sixteenth and seventeenth centuries. Now the trees have grown again, and from the churchyard there is a splendid view of the forest ridge.

BATEMAN'S

For almost three years Rudyard Kipling had been searching for the privacy and peace he needed when, in 1902, he saw Bateman's, hidden below the charming village of Burwash. In this new home he intended to abandon the Eastern tales which had already made him a famous writer, and concentrate on stories of English rural history and legend.

The house had been built in 1634 by a Sussex ironmaster when the Wealden iron industry was at its zenith. Kipling lived in it until his death in 1936, weaving it and the downland landscape into *Puck of Pook's Hill* and *Rewards and Fairies*. The old mill close by is found in *Traffics and Discoveries*, and in the wilderness beyond the rose garden and pond which Kipling laid out, flows the Dudwell stream, the 'Friendly Brook' of *A Diversity of Creatures*.

Inside, Bateman's is almost exactly as Kipling left it, and is now a National Trust property, open to the public.

THE BLUEBELL LINE

Floreat Vapor – 'Long Live Steam!' – is the motto of the last remaining steam railway in the county, the Bluebell Line.

When the Lewes-East Grinstead service of British Rail was discontinued in 1958 a determined band of steam enthusiasts immediately formed a preservation society and battled for funds to buy a portion of the line. Overcoming many difficulties they eventually acquired nearly five miles, linking a specially-built Bluebell Halt near Horsted Keynes with Sheffield Park Station. The first 'Bluebell Special' steamed triumphantly off in 1959, and the line was opened to public use the following year.

Thousands of passengers each summer enjoy riding in vintage rolling stock through lovely countryside and inspecting the growing outdoor museum of locomotives and other equipment from the steam age at the Sheffield Park terminus, close to which they can also delight in the Park itself, a showplace of beautiful and rare trees, shrubs and plants.

SHEFFIELD PARK
Nº 488

BODIAM CASTLE

Built soon after 1385 under royal licence by a veteran soldier, Sir Edward Dalyngridge, Bodiam (pronounced Bodjum) Castle was intended as a defence against French raiders on the River Rother. Its construction coincided with the end of castle building in England, and only twice did Bodiam have to withstand military assault.

After being besieged and taken by Parliament troops in the Civil War the castle was dismantled internally and left to decay. It was saved and restored by two widely different politicians in two later centuries: the eccentric 'Mad Jack' Fuller in the nineteenth century, and, in the twentieth, the former governor-general of India, the 1st Marquis Curzon, who left it to the nation at his death in 1926.

Externally, the castle retains its original appearance and, perfectly set off by its moat-lake, remains one of the country's most attractive castles – though merely a shell, for the 'slighted' interior has never been replaced.

PETWORTH HOUSE

The great post-Restoration wood carver Grinling Gibbons executed fine work in St. Paul's Cathedral, at Windsor, and in numerous famous houses; but connoisseurs agree that his finest achievement is this room named after him in Petworth House, which dominates the town of that name. His characteristic interweaving of flowers, fruits, animals, birds, fishes, musical instruments, foliage and lace is achieved with the utmost delicacy of craftsmanship and subtle effect.

His employer here, in 1692, was the Sixth Duke of Somerset, who by marriage had come into possession of the thirteenth century manor house, which he proceeded to incorporate into a grand new building. It later passed to the Earls of Egremont, who applied their taste and wealth to further improvements and added to the splendid collection of sculptures and paintings, ranging from old masters to the works of Turner, a frequent guest in this great mansion which, with its two thousand acres of park, is now National Trust property.

ALFRISTON

Alfriston parish church is 'The Cathedral of the Downs', so called because of its majestic proportions, with central shingled spire and soaring arches inside. It was built during the fourteenth century on the site of an earlier monastic church, in a field known as The Tye. Its adjoining Clergy House, of the same age, was the first building ever acquired by the National Trust, and has been restored to its original state.

But Alfriston's history has had many more secular features. This peaceful lane has sounded to the clop of hooves other than those of ponies being ridden for pleasure, for the village, situated where the Cuckmere bisects the line of the Downs, was for centuries a smugglers' haven, especially during the nineteenth century for the violent Alfriston Gang.

Its celebrated inn, The Star, dating from the fifteenth century, was usefully recognised at one time as a place of sanctuary for persons fleeing from the law.

EASTBOURNE

Eastbourne was originally known simply as Bourne, a name some of the older inhabitants continue to use: the stream, or bourne, still flows into the sea from a spring near the parish church of St. Mary. Old Eastbourne lies a mile inland, clustered around the church; and parts of this pleasantly dignified resort still maintain much of their village atmosphere. The Meades in particular is a little town in itself.

Eastbourne's fame really commenced with William Cavendish, Seventh Duke of Devonshire, who owned land in the area which he allowed to be developed after 1850. By the end of the century the place was fashionable and flourishing.

The colourful Carpet Gardens shown here lie behind the famous parade, flanked at its western end by the Wish Tower, a martello tower built as part of the coastal defence during the Napoleonic Wars. Beyond it towers Beachy Head, nearly 600 feet high, the eastern termination of the South Downs.

CHANCTONBURY

Sussex legend says that the ghost of a bearded Saxon warrior is to be seen at times on Chanctonbury searching for the treasure he had buried on the hill before his death at the Battle of Hastings.

Chanctonbury, above the village of Washington, commands a magnificent view of the surrounding South Downs; and on a clear day one can see as far north as Leith Hill in Surrey, while to the south is the sea beyond Cissbury. The hill is crowned with a grove of beech trees planted during the mid-eighteenth century by a schoolboy, Charles Goring, who lived at Wiston House near Washington. The grove is one of the most famous landmarks in the county.

It is not, as many people erroneously believe, the Chanctonbury Ring: this is the name given to an Iron Age hill fort below the grove, containing the ruins of later Roman buildings, including a Romano-British temple.

ARUNDEL

The overall visual affect of Arundel is arresting from almost any viewpoint, including vistas along the quieter streets of charming houses towards the great castle which dominates the busy town.

The castle was built soon after 1070 by Roger de Montgomerie on the site of an earlier stronghold guarding the River Arun, which takes its name from the town through which it flows – though there is still argument over the origin of the name, some believing it to be derived from Hirondelle, the horse of the legendary giant Bevis of Southampton who was warder of the gate-house during Norman times.

It was through the descendants of Queen Adeliza, widow of Henry I, that the castle eventually passed into the ownership of the Dukes of Norfolk, premier peers of England. It is still theirs, though the family home is now a modern house in the vast park. Castle and park are open to the public.

BRIGHTON ROYAL PAVILION

Many distinguished architects and designers had a hand in building and 'improving' Brighton's Royal Pavilion, but the supreme overseer was the Prince Regent (later King George IV), who wanted to create something unique at the fashionable watering-place his influence had transformed from a quiet fishing village. He succeeded, though the tastefulness or otherwise of his exotic Oriental fantasy was as much disputed in his time as it has been since – the clergyman-wit Sydney Smith remarked that the dome of St. Paul's had 'come to Brighton and pupped'.

Demolition threatened the Pavilion in the mid-nineteenth century, but Brighton Corporation bought it and it remains, fascinating in its external grotesqueness, yet useful as a concert and exhibition hall and conference place, and visited by many sightseers who find much to admire in the *chinoiserie* of the original decoration and the magnificent display of Regency furnishings, largely lent by H.M. the Queen.

BERWICK: VIEW OF THE DOWNS

Many parts of rural Sussex still look as they must have done centuries ago, as in this view of the South Downs from Berwick, an isolated hamlet standing beside the Cuckmere river, a little settlement which was old even before the Normans came.

The mighty ridge of the Downs, extending eastward out of Hampshire to terminate abruptly at Eastbourne, are the great glory of the county's scenery, their smooth slopes rising gently from the Weald, the wide expanse of flat farmland which they divide from the coastal strip and protect from Channel weather. Southdown sheep thrive on the slopes, though in lesser numbers than before the Second World War when the demands of crop-growing necessitated ploughing up sections of greensward. Here and there chequerboards of brown soil still show against the green of the Downs where arable farming has continued.

Otherwise, they remain unblemished, looming ancient and mysterious: Belloc's beloved 'great hills of the South Country'.

DITCHLING: ANNE OF CLEVES' HOUSE

'The Flanders Mare' was Henry VIII's description of his fourth wife, Anne of Cleves, whom he divorced in 1540 after only six months of marriage.

Anne was fortunate: she was taken care of in a far kinder way than several of Henry's other wives, being given a handsome pension and a number of estates in the country. During her 'retirement' she had two houses in Sussex, one at Southover near Lewes, and the picturesque sixteenth-century house shown here, at Ditchling.

The village lies at the foot of the South Downs below Ditchling Beacon, and was originally the administrative centre of a large Saxon royal estate belonging to Alfred the Great. Parts of the Church of St. Margaret, a cruciform building which stands opposite Anne of Cleves' House a little above one of the four narrow streets in this cross-shaped village, are believed to date back to late Saxon times.